The Digital Detox

How to Break free from your Screen Addiction

Riley Sterling

Table of contents

Chapter 1: Introduction

The rise of digital addiction

The rise of digital addiction has been a global phenomenon in recent years.

Smartphones, tablets, laptops, and other digital devices have become an integral part of our daily lives, and we often find ourselves glued to screens for hours on end.

While these devices have brought about significant benefits, such as improved communication and access to information, they have also led to a rise in digital addiction.

Digital addiction is a term used to describe the excessive use of digital devices, particularly smartphones and social media platforms.

It is characterized by a compulsive need to check notifications, browse social media, play games, and watch videos, among other activities.

Digital addiction has been linked to a range of negative effects, including poor mental health, decreased productivity, and social isolation.

One of the main drivers of digital addiction is the dopamine hit we receive from using our devices. Dopamine is a neurotransmitter that plays a critical role in the brain's reward system. When we engage in activities that stimulate the release of dopamine, such as scrolling through social media or playing a game, we feel a sense of pleasure and satisfaction.

Over time, our brains can become addicted to this feeling, leading to a compulsive need to engage in these activities.

Digital minimalism is a movement that seeks to counter the rise of digital addiction by promoting a more mindful and intentional use of digital devices.

It encourages individuals to be more deliberate about the apps they use, the notifications they receive, and the time they spend on their devices. By reducing the amount of time we spend on digital devices, we can break the cycle of addiction and improve our overall well-being. To break free from digital addiction, it is essential to take a digital detox.

A digital detox involves taking a break from all digital devices for a specified period.

This can be a few hours, a day, or even a week. During this time, individuals are encouraged to engage in offline activities such as reading, exercising, or spending time with loved ones. A digital detox can help break the cycle of addiction and allow individuals to reset their relationship with digital devices.

The rise of digital addiction is a significant challenge facing our society today.

However, by adopting the principles of digital minimalism and taking regular digital detoxes, individuals can break free from their screen addiction and improve their overall well-being. It is time for us to take control of our digital lives and embrace a more mindful and intentional approach to technology.

The impact of screen time on our health and relationships

The rise of technology has brought about a new era of convenience and connectivity. But with that convenience comes a price - the impact of screen time on our health and relationships.

Research shows that excessive screen time can lead to a range of health issues, including eye strain, headaches, and disrupted sleep patterns. The blue light emitted by screens can also disrupt the body's natural circadian rhythms, leading to fatigue and mood swings.

But the impact of screen time goes beyond physical health. It can also have a profound effect on our relationships. Spending too much time on our phones or laptops can lead to social isolation and a lack of meaningful connections with others.

It can also lead to a breakdown in communication, as we become more focused on our screens than on the people around us. For digital abusers, the impact of screen time can be particularly damaging.

Many of us have become so reliant on technology that we struggle to disconnect, even when we know it's in our best interest.

We may feel a sense of anxiety or restlessness when we're away from our screens, or we may find ourselves constantly checking our devices for notifications.

The good news is that it's never too late to break free from your screen addiction.

By adopting a digital minimalism approach, you can learn to use technology in a more intentional and mindful way.

This might involve setting boundaries around your screen time, such as turning off your phone during mealtimes or before bed.

It might also involve finding alternative ways to connect with others, such as engaging in hobbies or activities that don't involve screens.

By taking these steps, you can begin to reclaim your health and your relationships.

You'll be able to enjoy the benefits of technology without sacrificing your well-being or your connections with others.

So if you're ready to break free from your screen addiction, now is the time to take action.

The benefits of a digital detox

The benefits of a digital detox are numerous and significant.

They range from improved mental health and well-being to increased productivity and creativity. In this chapter, we will explore some of the most compelling advantages of taking a break from our screens. One of the most significant benefits of a digital detox is improved mental health. Research has shown that excessive screen time can lead to anxiety, depression, and other mental health issues.

By taking a break from our screens, we give our minds a chance to rest and recharge.

This can lead to greater clarity, improved mood, and better overall mental health.

Another benefit of a digital detox is increased productivity. When we spend less time on our screens, we have more time to focus on other activities. This can include work, hobbies, or spending time with loved ones. Additionally, research has shown that excessive screen time can actually decrease our productivity, as it can lead to distractions and a lack of focus.

In addition to improved mental health and productivity, a digital detox can also lead to increased creativity. When we spend less time consuming digital content, we have more time to create our own. This can include writing, drawing, or other artistic pursuits.

Additionally, a digital detox can help us to break free from the constraints of social media and other digital platforms, which can stifle our creativity and limit our ability to think outside the box.

Finally, a digital detox can help us to reconnect with the world around us. When we spend less time on our screens, we have more time to engage in real-world activities and connect with others. This can include spending time in nature, volunteering, or simply spending time with friends and family.

A digital detox offers numerous benefits for digital abusers and those interested in digital minimalism. From improved mental health and productivity to increased creativity and connection with the world around us, there are many compelling reasons to take a break from our screens. If you're feeling overwhelmed by your digital habits, consider taking a digital detox to reap these benefits and improve your overall well-being.

Chapter 2: Understanding Digital Addiction

What is digital addiction?

In today's fast-paced world, technology has become an integral part of our lives.

From smartphones to social media platforms, we rely on these digital devices and platforms for almost everything.

However, it's easy to get caught up in the digital world and become addicted to it.

Digital addiction is a growing problem that affects millions of people worldwide.

So what is digital addiction?

Simply put, it's the excessive use of digital devices and platforms that interferes with your daily life and causes negative consequences.

It's not just about spending too much time on your phone or computer; it's also about the emotional and psychological impact of your digital habits.

Digital addiction can manifest in different ways. For some, it's the constant need to check social media updates, even during important meetings or family gatherings.

For others, it's the compulsion to play online games for hours on end. Some people may even suffer from anxiety or depression when they are away from their digital devices.

The problem with digital addiction is that it can have serious consequences on our health and wellbeing. It can lead to sleep disorders, eye strain, and even physical problems like carpal tunnel syndrome. It can also affect our relationships with others, as we become more isolated and less present in the real world.

If you're a digital abuser, it's important to recognize the signs of digital addiction and take steps to break free from it.

This is where the principles of digital minimalism and mindfulness come in.

Digital minimalism involves reducing your digital footprint and using technology intentionally and mindfully.

Mindfulness, on the other hand, involves being present in the moment and fully engaging in your surroundings.

By practicing digital minimalism and mindfulness, you can regain control of your digital habits and improve your overall wellbeing. This may involve setting boundaries on your device usage, taking breaks from technology, and finding alternative ways to connect with others. With time and dedication, you can break free from your digital addiction and live a more balanced and fulfilling life.

The signs and symptoms of digital addiction

The signs and symptoms of digital addiction are often overlooked or ignored, but they can have a significant impact on our overall well-being and quality of life.

Digital addiction can manifest in a variety of ways, from compulsively checking social media to spending excessive amounts of time playing video games. One of the most common signs of digital addiction is the inability to control our use of technology. We may find ourselves constantly reaching for our phone or laptop, even when we know we should be doing something else. This can lead to feelings of guilt and shame, as well as a sense of being out of control.

Another symptom of digital addiction is the impact it has on our relationships. We may find ourselves neglecting our friends and family in favor of spending time online or playing video games. This can lead to feelings of isolation and loneliness, as well as strain on our personal and professional relationships.

Physical symptoms of digital addiction can include headaches, eye strain, and back pain from spending too much time sitting in front of a screen. We may also experience disrupted sleep patterns and a lack of energy, which can impact our overall health and well-being.

Mental health issues can also be a symptom of digital addiction. We may experience anxiety, depression, or other mental health issues as a result of our excessive use of technology.

This can be particularly true for those who use social media as a way to compare themselves to others, leading to feelings of inadequacy or low self-esteem.

Overall, the signs and symptoms of digital addiction can have a significant impact on our lives. If you find yourself struggling with these symptoms, it may be time to seek help and make a change. Digital minimalism is a great way to break free from your screen addiction and start living a happier, healthier life.

The psychology behind digital addiction
The psychology behind digital addiction is a complex and multifaceted issue.
In today's technology-driven world, it's easy to get hooked on our screens and devices.
There are several reasons why we become addicted to technology, and understanding them can help us break free.

One of the primary reasons for digital addiction is the release of dopamine in our brains. Dopamine is a neurotransmitter that plays a vital role in the pleasure and reward systems of the brain. When we engage with technology, whether it's scrolling through social media feeds or playing video games, our brain releases dopamine, creating a pleasurable sensation. This can lead to a cycle of seeking out more and more digital stimulation to achieve the same level of pleasure, leading to addiction.

Another reason for digital addiction is the fear of missing out (FOMO).

Social media platforms are designed to keep us engaged and connected, but they also create a sense of anxiety and pressure to be constantly connected. We fear missing out on important news, updates, and social interactions, leading us to constantly check our devices and stay connected.

Moreover, digital addiction can also be a coping mechanism for stress and anxiety. It's easy to get lost in the virtual world and escape from real-life problems, creating a temporary relief from stress and anxiety. However, this can lead to a cycle of avoidance, where individuals become increasingly reliant on technology to cope with their problems.

As digital abusers, it's essential to recognize the underlying psychological factors that contribute to addiction. Understanding these factors can help us develop strategies to break free from our screen addiction. Digital minimalism, a practice of simplifying our digital lives and reducing our dependence on technology, can be an effective way to combat digital addiction. By setting limits on our screen time, engaging in offline activities, and cultivating deeper connections with others, we can break free from the cycle of digital addiction and live a more fulfilling life.

Chapter 3: The Science of Digital Detox

The neurological effects of screen time and "mindfulness"

The rise of digital technology has brought a lot of benefits to our lives.

It has made communication easier, provided access to vast amounts of information, and allowed us to do things that were not possible before. However, it has also led to a rise in screen time, which has been linked to a range of neurological effects.

One of the most significant neurological effects of screen time is the impact it has on our sleep. The blue light emitted by screens can disrupt our circadian rhythm, making it harder for us to fall asleep at night.

This can lead to a range of problems, including insomnia, fatigue, and even depression.

Another neurological effect of screen time is the impact it has on our attention span.

Studies have shown that excessive screen time can lead to a decrease in our ability to focus and concentrate. This can lead to problems in school, work, and other areas of our lives. Screen time can also have an impact on our memory. Studies have shown that excessive screen time can lead to a decreased ability to remember things. This can be especially problematic for children, as their brains are still developing and they need to be able to remember things in order to learn.

Finally, excessive screen time can lead to an increase in anxiety and stress. The constant stimulation provided by screens can lead to a sense of overwhelm, which can lead to feelings of anxiety and stress.

In order to mitigate these neurological effects, it is important to reduce our screen time and engage in activities that promote mindfulness and digital minimalism. This can include things like meditation, spending time in nature, and engaging in activities that do not involve screens. By taking a more intentional approach to our screen time, we can reduce the negative neurological effects it can have on our lives and improve our overall well-being.

The Benefits of Unplugging

In today's world, it's almost impossible to go a day without being glued to a screen.

From smartphones to laptops, we have become so dependent on technology that we often forget to take a break.

This constant connection to our digital devices can have a negative impact on our physical and mental health. However, unplugging can provide several benefits that can help us improve our overall well-being.

Reduced Stress and Anxiety

Unplugging from technology can help reduce stress and anxiety levels.

The constant notifications and alerts from our devices can cause us to feel overwhelmed and anxious. Taking a break from technology can help us clear our minds and reduce our stress levels. This can lead to better sleep, improved mood, and a more relaxed state of mind.

Improved Focus and Productivity

When we unplug from technology, we can focus our attention on the present moment. This can help improve our productivity and creativity. Without the distractions of our devices, we can concentrate on the task at hand and get more done in less time.

Better Relationships

Unplugging can also improve our relationships with others. When we are constantly glued to our screens, we may not be fully present when spending time with loved ones.

By unplugging, we can be more engaged and attentive when spending time with others. This can help improve our relationships and strengthen our connections.

Increased Mindfulness

Unplugging can also help us become more mindful. When we are not constantly distracted by technology, we can focus on the present moment and become more aware of our thoughts and emotions.

This can help us become more self-aware and improve our overall well-being.

Unplugging from technology can provide several benefits that can help us improve our physical and mental health.

By taking a break from our devices, we can reduce stress and anxiety levels, improve focus and productivity, strengthen our relationships with others, and increase mindfulness.

So, the next time you feel overwhelmed by technology, take a break and unplug.

Your mind and body will thank you.

The science of behavior change

The science of behavior change is a complex field that involves understanding the factors that influence human behavior and how to modify it effectively. In the context of digital addiction, behavior change is particularly challenging because it involves breaking ingrained habits and patterns of behavior that have been reinforced over time.

One of the key concepts in behavior change is the idea of motivation.

Motivation is what drives us to take action and make changes, and it can come from both internal and external sources. For example, someone may be motivated to break their screen addiction because they want to improve their health and wellbeing, or because they want to be more productive at work.

Another important factor in behavior change is the environment. Our physical and social surroundings can have a significant impact on our behavior, and changing our environment can be a powerful tool for breaking bad habits. For example, removing screens from the bedroom or setting strict boundaries around screen time can help create a more conducive environment for healthy behavior.

One of the most effective strategies for behavior change is the use of rewards. Rewards can help reinforce positive behavior and create a sense of motivation and accomplishment. For example, someone might reward themselves with a favorite activity or treat after successfully completing a day without screens.

Finally, behavior change is a process that takes time and effort. It's important to be patient and persistent, and to be willing to try different strategies until you find what works best for you. With the right mindset and approach, anyone can break free from their screen addiction and live a more balanced and fulfilling life.

For digital minimalists, understanding the science of behavior change can be particularly helpful in maintaining their minimalist lifestyle. By understanding the factors that influence behavior, they can make intentional choices about their environment and habits, and stay motivated to stick to their minimalist principles. The science of behavior change is a powerful tool for breaking free from screen addiction and maintaining a minimalist lifestyle.

By understanding the factors that influence behavior, setting clear goals and rewards, and being patient and persistent, anyone can make positive changes in their life and live a more fulfilling and balanced existence.

Chapter 4: Planning Your Digital Detox

Assessing Your Screen Time Habits

In today's digital age, it's hard not to get sucked into the vortex of technology.

We rely on our smartphones, laptops, and tablets for everything from work to entertainment.

But have you ever stopped to think about how much time you spend staring at screens?

Do you find yourself mindlessly scrolling through social media, binge-watching Netflix, or checking your email every five minutes?

If so, it might be time to assess your screen time habits and make some changes.

The first step to breaking free from your screen addiction is to figure out how much time you're actually spending on your devices. Start by tracking your screen time for a week.

Most smartphones have a built-in feature that allows you to see how much time you spend on each app. Write down your usage for each app and total up your screen time at the end of the week. You might be surprised by how much time you're wasting on your devices.

Once you have a clear understanding of your screen time habits, it's time to evaluate what's essential and what's not. Ask yourself, "Do I need to check my email every hour, or can I wait until designated times during the day?" "Do I really need to spend two hours scrolling through Instagram, or can I limit my usage to 30 minutes a day?" By prioritizing the essential tasks and cutting back on the non-essential ones, you can reduce your screen time and improve your productivity.

Digital minimalism is a growing movement that emphasizes the importance of intentional technology use. It's not about eliminating technology altogether, but rather using it with purpose and intention. By adopting a digital minimalist lifestyle, you can reduce your screen time, increase your focus, and improve your mental health.

Here are a few tips for practicing digital minimalism:

1. Set boundaries: Establish specific times during the day when you allow yourself to use technology. For example, you might only check your email twice a day, or you might limit your social media usage to 30 minutes a day.

2. Unplug: Take regular breaks from technology. Go for a walk, read a book, or spend time with friends and family. Disconnecting from technology can help you recharge and improve your overall well-being.

3. Eliminate distractions: Turn off notifications on your phone and computer. By reducing the number of distractions, you can focus on the task at hand and improve your productivity. Assessing your screen time habits is the first step to breaking free from your screen addiction. By tracking your usage, evaluating what's essential, and adopting a digital minimalist lifestyle, you can reduce your screen time, increase your focus, and improve your overall well-being.

Setting goals for your digital detox

Setting goals for your digital detox is a crucial step towards breaking free from your screen addiction. Without clear and specific goals, it can be challenging to stay motivated and focused on your journey towards digital minimalism. Here are some tips to help you set effective goals for your digital detox:

1. Determine your why: Before setting any goals, it's essential to understand why you want to detox from your digital devices.

Is it to improve your mental health, be more present with loved ones, or increase productivity? Whatever your why may be, make sure it's meaningful and drives you towards achieving your goals.

2. Start small: It can be overwhelming to go from spending hours on your devices to completely cutting them off. Instead, start small by setting achievable goals such as reducing screen time by 30 minutes a day or turning off your phone during meals.

3. Be specific: Vague goals such as "spending less time on my phone" are challenging to measure and achieve. Instead, set specific goals such as "only checking social media twice a day" or "using my phone for work-related tasks only."

4. Use a tracking system: Tracking your progress can help you stay motivated and accountable. Use a digital detox app or a simple spreadsheet to track your daily screen time and progress towards your goals.

5. Reward yourself: Celebrate your achievements, no matter how small they may seem. Reward yourself with something you enjoy, such as a favorite meal or activity, for sticking to your goals.

Remember, setting goals for your digital detox is only the first step towards breaking free from your screen addiction. It's essential to stay committed to your goals and make gradual changes to your digital habits. With time and effort, you can achieve a healthier and more balanced relationship with your digital devices.

Creating a Digital Detox Plan

If you have realized that you are a digital abuser and want to break free from your screen addiction, creating a digital detox plan is the first step.

A digital detox plan is a set of guidelines that will help you reduce your screen time and increase your productivity, creativity, and overall well-being.

Here are some tips to create an effective digital detox plan:

1. Set Goals

The first step in creating a digital detox plan is to set goals. What do you want to achieve by reducing your screen time? Do you want to be more productive at work, spend more time with your family, or simply be more present in the moment? Write down your goals and make sure they are specific, measurable, achievable, relevant, and time-bound (SMART).

2. Identify Triggers

The next step is to identify your triggers for screen addiction. What activities or situations make you spend more time on your phone, tablet, or computer? Is it social media, email, gaming, or streaming? Once you know your triggers, you can find alternative activities or strategies to avoid or manage them.

3. Create Boundaries

The third step is to create boundaries for your screen time. How many hours per day or week do you want to spend on your devices? What times of the day or week do you want to be screen-free? What activities or places do you want to be screen-free? Communicate your boundaries to your family, friends, and colleagues and ask for their support.

4. Find Alternatives

The fourth step is to find alternatives to screen time. What activities or hobbies do you enjoy that don't involve screens? Do you like reading, writing, drawing, cooking, or exercising? Make a list of your favorite activities and schedule them into your daily or weekly routine.

5. Practice Self-Care

The fifth step is to practice self-care. Screen addiction can be a symptom of stress, anxiety, or depression. Take care of your physical, emotional, and mental health by getting enough sleep, eating well, exercising, meditating, or seeking professional help if needed.

Creating a digital detox plan requires self-awareness, discipline, and creativity.

By setting goals, identifying triggers, creating boundaries, finding alternatives, and practicing self-care, you can break free from your screen addiction and enjoy a more balanced and fulfilling life. If you need inspiration or support, join the digital minimalism community and share your journey with like-minded people.

Chapter 5: Building a Support System

Engaging your family and friends

Engaging your family and friends is one of the most important steps that you can take to break free from your screen addiction.

When you have the support of your loved ones, it becomes easier to stay motivated and focused on your goals.

Here are some tips to help you engage your family and friends in the digital detox process.

1. Explain your reasons for detoxing

Start by explaining the reasons why you want to detox from your screens. Be honest about the negative effects that screen addiction has had on your life and the benefits that you hope to gain from your digital detox. When your family and friends understand your motivations, they will be more likely to support you.

2. Set boundaries

It's important to set boundaries with your family and friends during your digital detox. Let them know when you will be disconnecting and when you will be available.

This can be challenging if you are used to being constantly connected, but it's important to stick to your boundaries to make the most of your detox.

3. Plan activities together

Plan activities with your family and friends that don't involve screens. This can be anything from going for a hike to playing board games. By spending time together without screens, you will strengthen your relationships and create new memories.

4. Encourage them to join you

Encourage your family and friends to join you in your digital detox. They may not be ready to commit to a full detox, but they may be willing to reduce their screen time. By working together, you can create a supportive environment that will make it easier for everyone to break free from their screen addiction.

5. Celebrate your successes

Finally, celebrate your successes with your family and friends. When you reach a milestone in your digital detox, let them know and celebrate together. By acknowledging your achievements, you will feel more motivated to continue with your detox.

Engaging your family and friends is an important part of the digital detox process.

By working together, you can create a supportive environment that will help you break free from your screen addiction and live a more fulfilling life.

Finding digital detox communities

In a world that is increasingly dominated by technology, it can be difficult to break away from your screens and disconnect from the digital world. However, for those who recognize the negative effects that excessive screen time can have on your mental and physical health, finding a community of like-minded individuals who prioritize digital detox and minimalism can be a valuable resource. Digital detox communities can offer a support system for individuals who are looking to reduce their screen time and adopt a more mindful approach to technology use.

These communities can be found both online and offline, and can range from social media groups to in-person meetups.

One great way to find digital detox communities is through social media platforms. Many individuals who are interested in digital minimalism have created groups on Facebook, Instagram, and other social networks to connect with others who share their values.

These groups can be a great place to share tips, offer support, and connect with others who are on a similar journey.

Another way to find digital detox communities is to look for local meetups and events.

Many cities have groups that organize regular meetups and events focused on digital minimalism and mindfulness.

These events can provide an opportunity to connect with others who are interested in reducing their screen time, and can offer a supportive environment to share experiences and tips. Finally, there are also a number of digital detox retreats and camps that offer a more immersive experience.

These retreats typically involve disconnecting from technology for an extended period of time, and can offer a chance to reset and recharge. While these retreats can be more expensive, they can be a valuable investment in your mental and physical well-being.

In summary, finding a community of individuals who prioritize digital minimalism and detox can be a valuable resource for those looking to break free from screen addiction. Whether through online groups, in-person meetups, or digital detox retreats, connecting with others who share your values can offer a supportive environment to help you achieve your goals.

Getting professional help

If you have tried to break free from your screen addiction and have been unsuccessful, it may be time to seek professional help.

There are many different types of professionals that can assist you in overcoming your addiction, including therapists, counselors, and addiction specialists.

Therapy can be an effective way to address underlying issues that may be contributing to your addiction. A therapist can help you identify the triggers that lead to your excessive screen use and develop strategies to manage them. They can also help you develop coping mechanisms for dealing with stress and anxiety that may be driving your addiction.

Counseling can also be helpful in addressing addiction. Addiction specialists can provide you with information on the nature of addiction and how it affects your brain and behavior. They can also provide you with practical tools to help you overcome your addiction, such as mindfulness techniques and behavioral therapies.

In addition to therapy and counseling, there are also a number of support groups available for those struggling with addiction.

These groups can provide an opportunity to connect with others who are going through similar struggles and provide a supportive environment for recovery.

Many of these groups are available online, making them accessible to those who may not be able to attend in-person meetings.

If you are considering seeking professional help for your addiction, it is important to do your research and find a qualified and experienced professional. Look for someone who specializes in addiction and has experience working with individuals who struggle with screen addiction.

Remember, breaking free from your screen addiction is a process, and it may take time and effort to overcome. However, with the right support and resources, it is possible to break free from your addiction and live a healthier, more balanced life.

Chapter 6: Implementing Your Digital Detox

Tips for Unplugging

In today's world, it's hard to imagine a day without digital devices. We spend hours scrolling through social media, binge-watching our favorite shows, and working on our laptops. While it's true that technology has made our lives easier, it has also led to a rise in screen addiction, causing us to lose touch with the real world.

If you're a digital abuser, you know how hard it is to put down your phone or step away from your computer. But it's important to take a break from technology every once in a while to rejuvenate your mind and body.

Here are some tips to help you unplug and reduce your screen time.

1. Set boundaries: Start by setting a limit on the amount of time you spend on your devices each day. This could be as simple as taking a break every hour to stretch your legs or as drastic as setting a time limit for social media apps.

2. Create a schedule: Plan your day in advance and allocate time for activities that don't involve technology. This could be anything from reading a book to practicing yoga.

3. Turn off notifications: Notifications can be distracting and cause you to pick up your phone unnecessarily. Turn off notifications for apps that you don't need to be constantly updated on.

4. Leave your phone at home: When you're out and about, try leaving your phone at home or in your bag. This will help you be more present in the moment and enjoy your surroundings.

5. Find a hobby: Engage in activities that don't require technology, such as drawing, gardening, or hiking. Not only will this help you unplug, but it will also help you discover new interests.

6. Use the "Do Not Disturb" mode: When you're trying to focus on a task, turn on the "Do Not Disturb" mode on your phone. This will prevent interruptions and help you stay on track.

7. Take a break: Sometimes, all you need is a break from technology. Take a day or weekend off from your devices and use the time to relax and recharge.

By following these tips, you can break free from your screen addiction and enjoy life beyond the digital world. Remember, digital minimalism is about finding balance and using technology in a way that enhances your life, not controls it.

Dealing with digital temptations

In today's world, we are surrounded by digital devices, and it's not always easy to resist the temptation to constantly check our phones, tablets, and computers.

Digital devices have become an integral part of our daily lives, and it's hard to imagine functioning without them. However, overuse of these devices can lead to addiction and negative consequences, including decreased productivity, unhealthy sleep patterns, and strained relationships. If you've found yourself struggling with digital temptations, you're not alone. There are many people who have recognized the negative impact of digital devices and have taken steps to reduce their usage.

Here are some tips to help you deal with digital temptations:

1. Set boundaries: One of the best ways to manage digital temptations is to establish clear boundaries. For example, you can set specific times of day when you will check your email or social media, or you can designate certain areas of your home as screen-free zones.

2. Use technology to your advantage: There are many apps available that can help you manage your screen time. For example, you can use an app that tracks your usage and sets limits on your screen time, or you can use a browser extension that blocks distracting websites.

3. Find alternative activities: One of the reasons we use digital devices so much is because we are bored or seeking entertainment. Instead of reaching for your phone, try finding alternative activities that you enjoy, such as reading, exercising, or spending time with friends and family.

4. Practice mindfulness: Mindfulness is the practice of being present and aware in the moment. By practicing mindfulness, you can become more aware of your thoughts and behaviors and make conscious decisions about your digital usage.

5. Seek support: If you're struggling with digital addiction, it can be helpful to seek support from friends, family, or a professional therapist. They can provide you with accountability and encouragement as you work to break free from your screen addiction.

By implementing these tips, you can start to manage your digital temptations and reduce your screen time. Remember, it's important to find a balance between digital usage and other activities that bring you joy and fulfillment. With a little effort, you can break free from your screen addiction and live a happier, healthier life.

Overcoming setbacks and relapses

In the journey of breaking free from screen addiction, setbacks and relapses are inevitable. Despite our best intentions, we may find ourselves slipping back into old habits and patterns. However, it's important to remember that setbacks and relapses are not signs of failure, but rather opportunities for growth and learning. One of the most effective ways to overcome setbacks and relapses is to have a support system in place. This can be in the form of friends, family, or even a support group of like-minded individuals.

Having someone to hold you accountable and provide encouragement can make all the difference in staying on track.

It's also important to identify the triggers that lead to relapses. This could be stress, boredom, or even a specific app or website.

Once you've identified your triggers, you can take steps to avoid or minimize them. For example, if social media is a trigger for you, consider deleting the app from your phone or setting strict time limits for usage.

Another helpful strategy is to focus on progress, not perfection. Breaking free from screen addiction is a process, and it's unlikely that you'll be able to completely eliminate all screen time overnight. Instead, celebrate small victories and focus on making gradual progress towards your goal.

Finally, don't be too hard on yourself if you do experience setbacks or relapses.

Remember that it's all part of the journey, and every step you take towards reducing your screen time is a step in the right direction.

For those practicing digital minimalism, setbacks and relapses can be especially challenging. The key is to stay focused on your values and priorities, and to use setbacks as an opportunity to reevaluate your relationship with technology. Ask yourself why you relapsed, and whether there are any adjustments you can make to your digital habits to prevent future relapses.

Setbacks and relapses are a natural part of the process of breaking free from screen addiction. By having a support system in place, identifying triggers, focusing on progress, and staying true to our values and priorities, we can overcome these challenges and continue on the path towards a healthier relationship with technology.

Chapter 7: The Benefits of a Digital Detox

Improved Physical Health

One of the most significant benefits of a digital detox is improved physical health. Digital abusers spend an average of 10 hours a day staring at screens, which can lead to a variety of health problems, including back pain, neck pain, headaches, eye strain, and poor posture. Additionally, the blue light emitted by screens can disrupt your sleep patterns, leading to fatigue and decreased productivity.

By taking a break from your screens, you can alleviate many of these physical health problems.

Here are some ways a digital detox can improve your physical health:

1. Better posture: When you're staring at a screen for hours on end, it's easy to hunch over and strain your neck and back. By taking a break from your screens, you can practice good posture and avoid these problems.

2. Less eye strain: The blue light emitted by screens can cause eye strain and dryness. By taking a break from your screens, you can give your eyes a break and reduce these symptoms.

3. Improved sleep: The blue light emitted by screens can disrupt your sleep patterns, leading to fatigue and decreased productivity. By taking a break from your screens, you can improve your sleep and feel more rested and energized.

4. Increased physical activity: When you're not staring at screens, you have more time to engage in physical activity. This can help you maintain a healthy weight, reduce your risk of chronic diseases, and improve your overall physical health.

5. Reduced stress: The constant stimulation of screens can lead to increased stress and anxiety. By taking a break from your screens, you can reduce your stress levels and improve your mental health.

Overall, a digital detox can have a significant impact on your physical health. By taking a break from your screens, you can alleviate many of the health problems associated with digital abuse and improve your overall well-being. So if you're a digital abuser looking to improve your physical health, consider taking a break from your screens and embracing digital minimalism.

Better mental health and well-being

In today's fast-paced world, it's no secret that we are all constantly connected to our screens. From smartphones to laptops, we spend hours each day scrolling through social media, checking emails, and watching videos.

While this constant connectivity has its benefits, it also has a significant impact on our mental health and well-being.

Digital abusers, those who are addicted to their screens, often suffer from anxiety, depression, and other mental health issues.

The constant stimulation and distraction that screens provide can leave us feeling overwhelmed and exhausted, making it difficult to focus on our work and personal lives.

Digital minimalism, on the other hand, is a movement that encourages us to reduce our reliance on technology and focus on the things that truly matter. By disconnecting from our screens, we can improve our mental health and well-being, allowing us to live more fulfilling and satisfying lives.

There are many ways that we can improve our mental health and well-being by disconnecting from our screens. Some of these include:

1. Taking breaks: We should take regular breaks from our screens throughout the day. This can help to reduce eye strain and fatigue, as well as improve our overall mood and productivity.

2. Engaging in physical activity: Regular exercise and physical activity can have a significant impact on our mental health and well-being. By disconnecting from our screens and engaging in physical activity, we can reduce stress, improve our mood, and boost our energy levels.

3. Practicing mindfulness: Mindfulness is a technique that involves focusing our attention on the present moment. By disconnecting from our screens and practicing mindfulness, we can reduce stress, improve our focus, and increase our overall sense of well-being.

4. Building healthy relationships: Our screens can often interfere with our ability to build and maintain healthy relationships. By disconnecting from our screens and spending time with friends and family, we can improve our social connections and increase our sense of happiness and well-being.

By disconnecting from our screens and focusing on our mental health and well-being, we can improve our overall quality of life. Whether you are a digital abuser or a digital minimalist, taking steps to reduce your screen time can have a significant impact on your mental health and well-being. So why not take the first step today and start your digital detox? Stronger relationships and social connections Stronger relationships and social connections are vital to our well-being, yet many of us struggle to maintain meaningful connections with others in today's digital age.

The constant barrage of notifications, emails, and social media updates can leave us feeling overwhelmed and disconnected from the people around us.

For digital abusers, this can be an especially challenging problem. Spending too much time online can lead to feelings of isolation and loneliness, which can negatively impact our mental health. Fortunately, there are steps we can take to strengthen our relationships and social connections, even in the midst of our digital lives. One of the most important things we can do is to prioritize face-to-face interactions with others.

While it's easy to rely on text messages and social media to stay in touch with friends and family, nothing can replace the value of spending time together in person.

Make a point to schedule regular meetups with people you care about, whether it's for a coffee date, a dinner party, or a weekend getaway.

Another way to strengthen your social connections is to get involved in your community. Volunteering, joining a hobby group, or attending local events are all great ways to meet new people and build meaningful relationships. Not only will this help you feel more connected to others, but it can also give you a sense of purpose and meaning in your life. Finally, it's important to be intentional about the time you spend online. Set boundaries for yourself and limit your screen time, so you can be fully present when you are with others. Turn off your phone during meals or when spending time with loved ones, and resist the urge to check your social media accounts constantly.

By prioritizing face-to-face interactions, getting involved in your community, and being intentional about your screen time, you can strengthen your relationships and social connections in a digital age. Remember, true connections with others require effort and intentionality, but the rewards are well worth it.

Chapter 8: Maintaining a Digital Minimalist Lifestyle

Strategies for Reducing Screen Time

If you are a digital abuser and want to reduce your screen time, there are several strategies you can implement to help you break free from your screen addiction.

Here are some tips to get you started:

1. Set Limits

One of the most effective ways to reduce your screen time is to set limits on how much time you spend on your devices. You can use apps like Moment or Freedom to track your screen time and set daily limits for yourself. This will help you become more aware of how much time you spend on your devices and give you an incentive to cut back.

2. Create Boundaries

Another way to reduce your screen time is to create boundaries around your device usage. For example, you can set a rule that you won't check your phone during meals or after a certain time in the evening. This will help you be more present in the moment and less distracted by your devices.

3. Practice Mindfulness

Mindfulness is a powerful tool for reducing screen time. When you practice mindfulness, you are more aware of your thoughts and feelings, which can help you identify when you are using your devices to avoid uncomfortable emotions. By practicing mindfulness, you can learn to sit with your emotions instead of numbing them with your devices.

4. Find Alternatives

One of the reasons we spend so much time on our devices is that we don't have other activities to fill our time. To reduce your screen time, try finding alternative activities that you enjoy. This could be anything from reading a book to going for a walk. The key is to find activities that you enjoy and that help you disconnect from your devices.

5. Create a Support System

Breaking free from your screen addiction can be challenging, but it's easier when you have a support system in place. This could be a friend or family member who is also trying to reduce their screen time, or it could be a support group for digital minimalists. Having a support system can help you stay accountable and motivated as you work to reduce your screen time.

Reducing screen time is essential for digital abusers who want to break free from their screen addiction. By setting limits, creating boundaries, practicing mindfulness, finding alternatives, and creating a support system, you can reduce your screen time and live a more balanced life.

Building Healthy Digital Habits

In today's digital age, it's easy to get caught up in the never-ending stream of notifications, emails, social media updates, and other distractions that come with our devices. However, it's important to remember that these devices are tools, not necessities, and that we have the power to control how we use them. In this section, we'll discuss some tips for building healthy digital habits that can help you break free from your screen addiction.

1. Set Boundaries: One of the most important things you can do to build healthy digital habits is to set boundaries for yourself. This means deciding when and how you will use your devices. For example, you might decide to turn off your phone during meals, or to only check social media once a day. By setting clear boundaries, you'll be able to focus on the things that matter most to you.

2. Practice Mindfulness: Mindfulness is the practice of being present in the moment and paying attention to your thoughts and feelings without judgment. When it comes to building healthy digital habits, mindfulness can help you become more aware of how you're using your devices and the impact they're having on your life. By practicing mindfulness, you'll be able to make more intentional choices about how you use your devices.

3. Take Breaks: It's important to take breaks from your devices throughout the day. This can help you recharge your batteries and prevent burnout. Try taking a walk, reading a book, or engaging in other activities that don't involve screens. By taking breaks, you'll be able to stay more focused and productive when you do use your devices.

4. Prioritize Sleep: Sleep is essential for our physical and mental health. However, many of us sacrifice sleep in favor of spending more time on our devices. To build healthy digital habits, it's important to prioritize sleep and create a bedtime routine that doesn't involve screens. This can help you get better quality sleep and wake up feeling more refreshed.

5. Practice Digital Minimalism: Digital minimalism is the practice of using technology in a way that adds value to your life, while minimizing the negative effects. This means being intentional about the apps, websites, and other digital tools you use, and cutting out anything that doesn't serve a purpose. By practicing digital minimalism, you'll be able to create a healthier relationship with your devices.

By following these tips, you can start building healthy digital habits that will help you break free from your screen addiction. Remember, it's never too late to make a change, and small habits can lead to big results over time.

So, take control of your devices, and start living a more intentional and mindful life today!

Living a More Intentional Life

In today's fast-paced and digitally driven world, it's easy to get distracted by the never-ending stream of notifications and information coming from our devices. However, all this digital noise can leave us feeling overwhelmed, stressed, and disconnected from the world around us.

If you're someone who feels like your digital habits are taking over your life, it's time to start living more intentionally. This means being deliberate and purposeful in everything you do, from the way you spend your time to the relationships you cultivate.

Here are some tips for living a more intentional life:

1. Set Goals and Priorities

To live intentionally, you need to know what's important to you. Take some time to reflect on your values and what you want to achieve in life. Then, set goals that align with these priorities.

For example, if you value spending time with loved ones, make it a priority to schedule regular family dinners or weekend outings. If you want to advance in your career, set goals for professional development and take steps to achieve them.

2. Create Boundaries

Digital devices can easily blur the lines between work and personal life, leading to burnout and stress. To live more intentionally, create boundaries around your digital use.

For example, set specific times of the day when you check your emails or social media. Turn off notifications during non-work hours and prioritize time for self-care and relaxation.

3. Practice Mindfulness

Mindfulness is the practice of being present and fully engaged in the current moment. When you're mindful, you're able to tune out distractions and focus on what's happening right now.

To incorporate mindfulness into your daily routine, try practicing meditation or deep breathing exercises. Take breaks throughout the day to check in with yourself and recenter your focus.

4. Cultivate Meaningful Relationships

Living intentionally also means cultivating meaningful relationships with the people in your life. This means making time for face-to-face interactions and prioritizing the people who matter most to you.

Make an effort to schedule regular outings with friends and family members. Reach out to old friends and acquaintances and reconnect over shared interests.

By living more intentionally, you can break free from the digital distractions that are holding you back and start living a more fulfilling and purposeful life. So, take the first step today and start making intentional choices that align with your values and goals.

Chapter 9: Conclusion

Reflecting on your digital detox journey

Congratulations, you have made it this far! You have taken the first step towards breaking free from your screen addiction.

You have recognized that your digital habits were negatively impacting your life and decided to take action. You have successfully completed your digital detox journey, and now it is time to reflect on what you have learned.

Reflecting on your digital detox journey is an essential step in maintaining your newfound digital minimalism lifestyle. It allows you to understand what worked for you, what didn't, and how you can continue to improve.

Here are some tips that can help you reflect on your journey:

1. Take a moment to celebrate your success

You have completed your digital detox journey, and that is something to be proud of.

Take a moment to celebrate your success and acknowledge the hard work you put in to get here. It is essential to recognize your achievements and to use them as motivation to continue your digital minimalism journey.

2. Evaluate your digital habits

Reflect on your digital habits before, during, and after your detox journey. It will help you identify your triggers, understand your patterns and develop a plan to prevent relapse.

Ask yourself questions like: What were your most significant challenges? What did you miss the most about your digital devices? What new habits did you develop during your detox journey?

3. Set new goals

Now that you have completed your digital detox journey, it is time to set new goals. What are your digital minimalism goals? Do you want to reduce your screen time further? Do you want to develop new habits to support your digital minimalism lifestyle? Whatever your goals may be, make sure they are specific, measurable, attainable, relevant, and time-bound.

4. Create a plan

Develop a plan to achieve your digital minimalism goals. It could be a daily routine, a weekly schedule, or a monthly plan. Make sure your plan is realistic, and it aligns with your goals. Don't forget to include strategies to overcome roadblocks and prevent relapse.

Reflecting on your digital detox journey is an essential step in maintaining your digital minimalism lifestyle. It allows you to evaluate your digital habits, set new goals, and create a plan to achieve them. Remember, your digital detox journey is not a one-time event, but a lifestyle change. Keep up the good work, and you will soon reap the benefits of a digital minimalism lifestyle.Celebrating your progress Celebrating your progress is an essential step in your journey towards digital minimalism. As you start to reduce your screen time and break free from your digital addiction, it is important to acknowledge your accomplishments and take pride in your progress.

By celebrating your progress, you are motivating yourself to continue on the path towards a healthier digital lifestyle. It is easy to get discouraged and feel like you are not making any progress, especially when you are trying to break a habit that has been a part of your life for a long time.

Celebrating your progress can help you stay focused and committed to your goals.

One way to celebrate your progress is to keep a journal or a log of your screen time.

Write down how much time you spend on your devices each day and track your progress as you start to reduce your screen time.

When you reach a milestone, such as going a whole day without checking your phone, take a moment to celebrate your accomplishment.

Treat yourself to a nice meal or buy yourself a small gift as a reward for your hard work.

Another way to celebrate your progress is to share your journey with others. Join a support group or online community of digital minimalists and share your successes and challenges with others. Celebrate each other's accomplishments and encourage each other to continue on the path towards a healthier digital lifestyle.

Remember, celebrating your progress is not about being perfect or reaching a specific goal. It is about acknowledging the small steps you are taking towards a healthier digital lifestyle and taking pride in your accomplishments.

By celebrating your progress, you are building the confidence and motivation you need to continue on the path towards a more balanced and fulfilling life.Embracing a mindful, minimalist lifestyle

Embracing a mindful, minimalist lifestyle is all about slowing down and simplifying your life. In our fast-paced, technology-driven world, it can be easy to get caught up in the constant stream of notifications, emails, and social media updates. However, by adopting a mindful, minimalist lifestyle, you can break free from the cycle of digital addiction and rediscover the joys of living in the present moment.

At its core, digital minimalism is about using technology in a purposeful way, rather than mindlessly scrolling through your phone or checking your email every five minutes.

By setting clear boundaries and prioritizing your time, you can create more space for the things that truly matter in your life.

One of the key principles of a mindful, minimalist lifestyle is to focus on quality over quantity. Instead of constantly seeking out new experiences and possessions, try to cultivate a deeper appreciation for the things you already have. This can include things like spending time with loved ones, practicing gratitude, and engaging in activities that bring you joy and fulfillment. Another important aspect of digital minimalism is to be mindful of the impact that technology is having on your mental health and wellbeing. This can include things like taking regular breaks from your devices, practicing mindfulness meditation, and prioritizing self-care activities like exercise, healthy eating, and sleep.

Ultimately, embracing a mindful, minimalist lifestyle is all about finding balance in a world that is increasingly dominated by technology. By focusing on what truly matters and being intentional with your time and energy, you can break free from the cycle of digital addiction and live a more fulfilling, meaningful life.

About the author

Riley Sterling is a captivating voice in the realm of personal growth and digital wellness.

With a deep understanding of the perils of modern-day screen addiction, Riley embarked on a personal journey to find balance and reclaim a life free from the grips of technology. Through extensive research and personal experiences, Riley has become a trusted expert in the field, empowering individuals to break free from the shackles of screen addiction and embrace the liberating power of a digital detox. Through their inspiring writing, Riley shares practical strategies and transformative insights to help readers reclaim their focus, find authentic connections, and cultivate a healthier relationship with technology.

With 'The Digital Detox: How to Break Free from Your Screen Addiction,' Riley Sterling invites readers on a life-changing journey towards a more mindful and intentional existence in the digital age.